DATE DUE

T. SHA A1		
DORR 9		
BUTTE B 2		
DORR H 3 2		
MONTA B 1 9 '86		
BOGUS B 1 1 9 90		
SEP 3 0 1997		
SEP 0 8 1998		
SEP 2 1 1999 4th		
OCT 5 - 2005		

D1008875

17315

YOU AND YOUR PET
Horses

You and Your Pet
Horses

PHIL STEINBERG

Illustrations by DIANA MAGNUSON

 Lerner Publications Company
Minneapolis

Front cover photo courtesy of Webb AgPhotos.
Back cover photo by E. Lempereur. © 1969 by Librairie A. Hatier.

LIBRARY OF CONGRESS CATALOGING IN PUBLICATION DATA

Steinberg, Phillip Orso.
  Horses.

  (You and Your Pet)
  Includes index.
  SUMMARY: Discusses the breeds and general characteristics
of horses, learning to ride, feeding, grooming, and general care
and gives a brief history of the horse.

  1. Horses—Juvenile literature. [1. Horses] I. Magnuson,
Diana. II. Title. III. Series.

SF302.S73 1978   636.1   78-54355
ISBN 0-8225-1257-2

Manufactured in the United States of America. Published
simultaneously in Canada by J. M. Dent & Sons (Canada) Ltd.,
Don Mills, Ontario.

International Standard Book Number: 0-8225-1257-2
Library of Congress Catalog Card Number: 78-54355

1 2 3 4 5 6 7 8 9 10 85 84 83 82 81 80 79 78

CONTENTS

AN ANCIENT PARTNERSHIP

Horses and human beings have long been partners in the struggle for survival. No one knows exactly when people stopped hunting the horse for meat and began using it as a pack animal. Its great strength, no doubt, convinced early people that it was an animal good for packing, hauling, and pulling. And its superior speed gave hunters an advantage over the game they chased.

When people stopped hunting for their food and began growing it instead, the horse readily changed from its role as fleet hunter to sturdy plow animal. And when people put aside the plow to go to war, their horses carried them into battle. History has since shown that when tribes or nations fought each other, the side with the most horses and the best riders usually won.

As late as the 1880s, blacksmith shops and livery stables were as common in the United States as gas stations are today. Horses were so widely used that horse-stealing was considered one of the worst crimes anyone could commit.

But by the 1920s, the smell of gasoline and oil began replacing the smell of hay and leather. With the increasing use of the gasoline engine, people stopped using the horse for transportation, farming, and waging war. Instead they turned to more efficient "iron horses"— the automobile, the tractor, and the tank.

Because of the machine age, many people thought the horse had outlived its usefulness. Some even thought it would meet with extinction. Wild horses, as late as 1971, were hunted for their meat, which went into pet foods. (Wild herds are now protected by law.)

Today, however, there are more than eight million horses in the United States. People interested in pleasure riding, racing, and breeding horses have placed a new value on the animal that has served humanity so well. The horse has become an animal used for pleasure and appreciated for its beauty, fleetness, and intelligence.

THE ORIGIN OF THE HORSE

Scientists believe horses were living on earth as long as 50 million years before the first human beings. These beliefs are based on fossil remains discovered in various parts of the world.

In 1838, part of a curious-looking jawbone was unearthed in a backyard in England. Experts on fossils, called *paleontologists* (pay-lee-uhn-TAHL-uh-jists), became excited about this particular fossil. They examined the bone and decided it was the jaw of a monkey. A few months later, another jawbone like the first was dug up in another part of England. This bone contained an almost complete set of teeth. The scientists studied the bone and its tiny teeth and decided it was not the jaw of a monkey at all but a part of the skull of some small extinct animal.

About 30 years later a bone similar to the English bones was dug up in the southwestern United States. Scientists thought this bone, too, might be part of a monkey skull. Upon closer examination, they found that the small jawbone closely resembled the bones the English scientists had found. The American scientists claimed that the jaw of this little animal once belonged to an ancestor of the horse. They called this animal *Eohippus* (ee-oh-HIP-us). *Eo* is the Greek word for "dawn" or "beginning," and *hippus* means "horse."

The dawn horse was about the size of a fox. Its long head had small ears. It had four padded toes on each front foot and three padded toes on each back foot. Its legs were quite short.

At the time of the dawn horse, the earth was covered with swamps and tropical forests. Giant crocodiles and lizards wallowed in the murky waters, and huge ferns rose up around the tall trees. *Eohippus* nibbled these ferns. When chased by flesh-eating, wolf-like animals, the dawn horse hid in the thick vegetation.

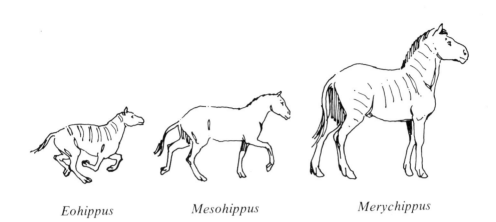

Eohippus   *Mesohippus*   *Merychippus*

In the millions of years following the era of the dawn horse, many changes came over the earth. The swamps dried up and were replaced by broad plains. The jungle-like forests thinned, mountains formed, and the climate cooled. And, as the appearance of the earth changed, so did that of each animal living on it. The dawn horse grew to the size of a sheep. Its eyes were larger and set farther apart. Its legs grew longer and, through the ages, it lost a toe on each foot. Scientists call this later animal *Mesohippus* (mez-oh-HIP-us), or "middle horse."

A few more million years brought more changes to the appearance of the little horse. It grew to be the size of the present-day Shetland pony. It no longer had to hide from its enemies because it could outrun them. And with no more swamps and ferns, it had to change its eating habits. It grazed on the lush grass that covered the plains. Scientists call this animal *Merychippus* (mare-ik-HIP-us), meaning a "grass-eating" or "cud-chewing horse."

10

Pliohippus   *Equus*

During the next ten million years, the ancestor of the horse grew to the height of today's donkey, and the hair on the top of its neck developed into a stiff mane. The eyes of this animal were set still more widely apart, thus widening its range of vision. The structure of its foot changed the most. Its outside toes had practically disappeared, while the middle toe grew strong and wide. Scientists call this one-toed horse *Pliohippus* (ply-oh-HIP-us), which means "more recent horse."

The last animal in the evolution of the horse was *Equus* (EH-kwoos), the "true horse." *Equus* was much stronger and larger than *Pliohippus*. Its large middle toe developed into a strong hoof and its long, muscular legs were capable of running at great speeds.

In 50 million years the dawn horse had changed from a small fox-sized creature to *Equus*, a tall, stout animal of exceptional strength. The most significant change was in the construction of the feet. The four-toed dawn horse was small and light; it may have spread its toes to help it walk on boggy surfaces. But as the marshy

11

swamps changed to dry plains, the horse's toed foot changed to a broad, hard hoof. All horses today are descendants of *Equus*, the true horse.

For millions of years *Equus* ran free and wild. It lived in small herds and moved in search of water and grazing land. Like the buffalo, it was hunted by early humans, perhaps as recently as twenty thousand years ago. Many more years passed before primitive people realized that *Equus* could be domesticated and used as a pack animal. How they made this discovery can only be a matter of speculation.

WILD HORSES

Today few horses run wild and free. The horses that do are descendants of the wild horses the cave dwellers failed to capture and tame. Different branches of the horse family developed from these animals. Their descendants closely resemble today's riding horses but are not the same. One of these wild horses is the Przhevalski's (pur-zheh-VAL-skeez) horse. It lives on the dry plains of Mongolia. This small, woolly horse was named after the Russian explorer who, in 1881, found the skin and skull of one of these animals in central Asia. The tribes of people that wander through the Gobi Desert have tried unsuccessfully to tame this creature.

Another wild relative of the horse is the onager

Przhevalski's horses

(AHN-uh-jur), which lives in remote parts of Asia. With its slick coat and long legs, the onager is much prettier than the Przhevalski's horse. Its big ears and tufted tail make it look much like a mule, but it is not. It is a distinct member of the family of wild horses. Because onagers have been hunted for their meat, they are almost extinct.

The wild ass of Africa is another relative of the horse and is the ancestor of the donkey. Wild asses live in small herds in northwestern Africa. With their huge ears and tufted tails, they look very much like the domesticated donkeys of the United States.

The zebra is still another kind of wild horse. Zebras are a breed of horse never tamed by humans. These animals can be found in many parts of Africa.

The so-called wild horses of the western United States, sometimes called mustangs, are not actually wild horses. They are horses whose once-tame ancestors escaped and became wild again. The only truly wild horses are the Przhevalski's horse, the onager, the wild ass, and the zebra.

HOW DOMESTICATED HORSES REACHED AMERICA

Skeletons found in many parts of the United States prove that the dawn horse and its ancestors once lived on the North American continent. Yet, when Columbus landed in the New World, there was not a single horse on the entire continent. What became of all the horses? Scientists believe that ages ago a bridge of land connected what is now Alaska to Russia. Many horses used this land bridge to leave the continent. The bridge later was worn away by the sea.

A change in climate may have been responsible for the horses' migration. Scientists believe that almost two million years ago, part of the earth became a frozen wasteland. This period of time is known as the Ice Age. Quite possibly, horses left the North American continent to search for food and to get away from the icy climate. Those that did not migrate died. From the time of the Ice Age to about 400 years ago, there was not one living horse on the North American continent.

The first domesticated horses were brought to the western hemisphere by Spanish explorers shortly after Columbus discovered the New World. As a result of the discovery, the king of Spain sent three expeditions to conquer and colonize the new lands. Don Hernando Cortes was the leader of the first expedition in 1519. He brought 16 horses with him.

At first, Cortes and his men were friendly with the Aztec Indians they met in the New World. But once the Spaniards saw all the gold and precious gems the Indians possessed, they became greedy. They decided to take these riches away from the Indians. Even though there were a thousand Indians to every Spaniard, the Spaniards overcame them. Cortes and his soldiers had guns, while the Indians had only slingshots and bows and arrows. But more importantly, the Spaniards had horses. This was the first time the Indians had seen horses. They were terrified by the strange monsters. Their religious beliefs made them think the Spaniards mounted on horses were powerful gods, and as a result, the Indians let themselves be conquered. In a letter to the king of Spain, Cortes wrote: "We owe our victory to the horses."

The second expedition was led by Hernando de Soto. Knowing that horses had meant victory for Cortes,

de Soto brought 250 horses with him to Florida. Like the Aztecs, the Florida Indians were frightened by the soldiers mounted on horses, and their fear contributed to de Soto's victories.

A third explorer, Francisco Coronado, came to New Mexico with 1,500 horses. The Indians he met were also terrified by the horses. But during battles with Coronado, the Indians realized that the Spanish warriors were just people and that the horses were just animals. Their arrows could kill both human and beast. They overcame their fear of horses.

Indians then began capturing runaway horses. They found that they, too, could master and ride these powerful animals. Soon the Indians became expert riders, controlling their animals without spurs or whips. Riding bareback, they rode as if they and their horses were one. When strays or runaways could not be found, the Indians stole horses. They gradually increased the numbers of their herds until they were able to halt their enemies' progress. The Spaniards had used horses to conquer the Indians; now the Indians used horses to drive back the Spaniards.

BREEDS OF HORSES

When knighthood was in full flower, a calm and steady horse was bred for the sole purpose of carrying an armor-clad knight in jousting tournaments. This huge horse needed great strength to bear the weight of its own heavy armor and that of the knight. A knight usually had another horse called a courser. This smaller, faster horse carried the knight into battle. Its quickness and spirit made up for its lack of bulk and strength.

Small, fast horses were bred mostly in the Orient. Because they had fiery temperaments, they were considered "hot-blooded." Large, heavy horses came mostly from Europe. Because they were calm and even-tempered, they were called "cold-blooded." Mixtures of these two strains gave rise to more than 60 different breeds of horses ranging in size from the tiny Shetland pony to the huge Clydesdale. Thus, the purpose of breeding different kinds of horses was to produce animals for special uses, such as cart-pulling or racing.

Hot-Blooded Horses

Of the hot-blooded horses, the Arabian is the best known. the Arabian is the oldest breed of purebred horse. Although it has been bred in Arabia for more than two thousand years, it probably originated somewhere along the northern coast of Africa. The Arabian, with its "dish," or concave, face and fine arched neck, is sometimes considered the most beautiful of all horses. It makes an excellent parade horse or cow pony. Although the Arabian is a good riding horse, it is not recommended for children. Its high spirit and nervousness demand the control of an experienced rider.

The Barb originated on the Barbary Coast of northern Africa. It is similar to the Arabian, but tends to be coarser and chunkier in appearance. Its exceptional intelligence and reliability make it an excellent cavalry or war horse. It sure-footedness makes it a good mountain horse. The crossbreeding of Arabians and Barbs has produced many fine mounts.

The horses brought to the New World by the Spaniards had both Arabian and Barb blood. They were strong, spirited horses with great endurance. Many of these horses fell into the hands of the Indians. Although the Indians were expert riders, they knew little about breeding horses. They were interested more in increasing the numbers of their herds than in improving the quality of their stock. The two million horses resulting from this casual breeding were called cayuses (KY-yoos-es). They were scrubby-looking range horses. But, because of their Arabian-Barb blood, they were rugged and high-spirited. The cowboys later called these horses mustangs. *Mustang* is a Mexican-Spanish word meaning "mixed" or "strayed." A bronco is a mustang that has not yet been broken. In other words, it is not used to the saddle and thus cannot be ridden.

Another of the hot-blooded breeds is the Thoroughbred. A Thoroughbred is a particular breed of horse that was bred to run fast. This breed originated in England more than 200 years ago when three oriental *stallions* (males)—a Barb, an Arabian, and a saddle horse—were mated with English *mares* (females). All Thoroughbreds today are descendants of the three oriental stallions and the English mares.

While most horses take more than four minutes to run a mile, a good Thoroughbred can run that distance in less than two minutes. A racing Thoroughbred tends to be nervous as well as fast. Only a well-trained jockey can handle a horse as sensitive as the Thoroughbred.

At the time the Thoroughbred was being developed, there were many people who liked to ride and hunt.

Arabian

Thoroughbred

Mustang

Clydesdale

They wanted a horse somewhat like the Thoroughbred, but they also wanted a bigger animal with a better disposition. The half-bred was the answer. A half-bred is a horse whose father or mother is a Thoroughbred and whose other parent is a working breed.

Cold-Blooded Horses

While fiery mustangs were the workhorses of the cowboys in the American west, heavy draft horses were the workhorses of the east. These enormous, cold-blooded horses are still used today. Like their ancestors, they are powerful, heavy animals, with each adult weighing more than 2,000 pounds (900 kilograms).

The calm and gentle Belgian is undoubtedly the strongest of the four draft breeds. In the past, it was used for pulling logs and heavy farm equipment. The Belgian's mane sometimes is a light blond color called "flaxen."

The Percheron is another giant of the cold-blooded breeds. This gray horse originated in France and is the most spirited of all drafters. Years ago it pulled coaches in Europe. Today the Percheron is the favorite performing horse of the circus.

The Clydesdale is a large beauty that originated in Scotland. It is still the only draft horse used in that country. The Clydesdale has fine, silky hair below its knees, referred to as "feathers," which makes it the most stylish of the draft horses. It moves along at a jaunty pace, lifting its feet high in the air. This "heather step" makes the Clydesdale look like a show horse even while it is pulling a plow in a farmer's field. A team of these showy horses pulling a fancy wagon is an unforgettable sight.

The biggest of all drafters is the English Shire. It is a slow-moving horse of great strength. Thick, coarse hair below the Shire's knees helps protect its legs. Shires are often crossbred with other workhorses to improve the size and strength of the smaller animals. Shires are still used for hauling logs, pulling stumps, and farming in the marshlands of England.

Crossbreeds

By crossbreeding speedy hot-blooded horses with strong cold-blooded horses, horse fanciers developed new "warm-blooded" breeds. The warm-blooded horses combine the strength of the draft horse with the speed and fire of the lighter horse. One of these crossbreeds is the hackney, a cross between a Thoroughbred and a cart horse known as the Norfolk Trotter. The hackney, an elegant animal with a smart step, lifts its knees halfway to its chin. This lively action and the hackney's bobbed tail are its trademarks. In England these horses once pulled coaches called hackneys. Today hackney ponies and horses are seen in most horse shows and in harness racing, a form of racing that uses a lightweight cart. The most popular hackneys are pony-sized.

In colonial North America, English pacers and Spanish jennets were bred to produce another warm-blooded variety. This crossbreeding resulted in an animal that is part workhorse and part racehorse. It has fast pick-up and is capable of unbelievably sudden turns and quick stops. For a distance of a quarter mile (about half a kilometer), no horse, including the Thoroughbred, is swifter. This remarkable horse is the American quarter horse. It gets its name from the exceptional speed it shows for a quarter mile.

Two other famous crossbreeds are the Morgan horse and the American saddle horse. The Morgan is named after Justin Morgan, a New England schoolteacher who, late in the 1700s, bought a small bay stallion of unknown origin. This proud animal could pull logs, jump fences, or carry a rider all day. The horse sired several strong, speedy beauties, thus founding the Morgan line, a popular breed in the United States today.

The American saddle horse was developed by pioneers who needed an animal capable of carrying one or two people comfortably for a long distance. This medium-sized horse is a mixture of many breeds. It has some of the fire and speed of the Thoroughbred, the easy gait of the Spanish horse, and the endurance and calmness of the Morgan. A frequent winner at horse shows, the American saddle horse is a mount that people own simply for the pleasure of riding.

Ponies

Some people mistakenly think that ponies are young horses. Baby horses are called *foals*. Male foals are called *colts* and female foals are called *fillies*. A pony is actually a smaller grown-up member of the horse family. The size of the adult animal is what determines if it is a horse or a pony.

Years ago when people wanted to measure the height of a horse, they did not use a ruler or yardstick. Instead they used the human hand as a unit of measure. A "hand" is four inches (10 centimeters). Any full-grown horse not more than 14.2 hands (14 hands and 2 inches) at the "withers" is a pony. (The ridge between the shoulders is the withers.)

Ponies, like other horses, are descendants of *Eohippus*, the dawn horse. Scientists believe the smallness of the pony in comparison to other adult horses is due to the fact that ponies evolved in cold, barren parts of the world. Because of the severe climate in these wastelands, there was little lush grass for grazing. The wild ponies living there had to spend most of their time searching for food. During the winter they often went hungry. Because of the scarcity of food, descendants of these animals never developed to the size of the horses living in milder climates.

Going without food helped ponies develop an endurance that other horses do not have. Because of the cold climate, the ponies' coats grew thick and heavy. And the hilly country in which the ponies lived gave them a sure-footedness almost equal to that of mountain goats. All these factors account for the pony's natural sturdiness and long life span. Ponies live longer than other horses. Some live to be more than 40 years old, which is a ripe old age, considering that the average life span of a horse is 25 years. Ponies generally are considered more intelligent and less nervous than other horses.

Today there are many breeds of ponies. The best known is the Shetland pony. It is native to the rugged Shetland Isles near the Arctic Circle. The Shetland pony was bred to be a small draft horse. The Scottish islanders used it for hauling loads of peat, a material they needed for fuel. Because of its size, the Shetland pony also was used by the English and Welsh for pulling carts in coal mines. Even though this pony was not bred to be a riding animal, it is now popular with children because of its size and gentleness. Though it is an intelligent, friendly animal, it tends to be stubborn.

The Dartmoor is a pony originally bred on the moors of southwestern England. It is a hardy, sure-footed animal that averages 12-1/2 hands, or 50 inches (125 centimeters), at the withers.

The Highland pony originated in Scotland. It, too, is a good riding pony, ranging in height from 50 to 56 inches (125 to 140 centimeters).

The Timor pony of Australia and New Zealand has

a chocolate coat speckled with cream-colored spots. Its mane and tail are also cream-colored.

The hackney pony, which originated in England, has strong hind legs that make it an excellent jumper. It is most popular, however, as a harness pony.

The Connemara is a pony originating in the heathery crags and bogs of Ireland. This pony is lion-hearted but gentle. The Connemara is an excellent jumper. Some have jumped fences more than six and a half feet (almost two meters) in height.

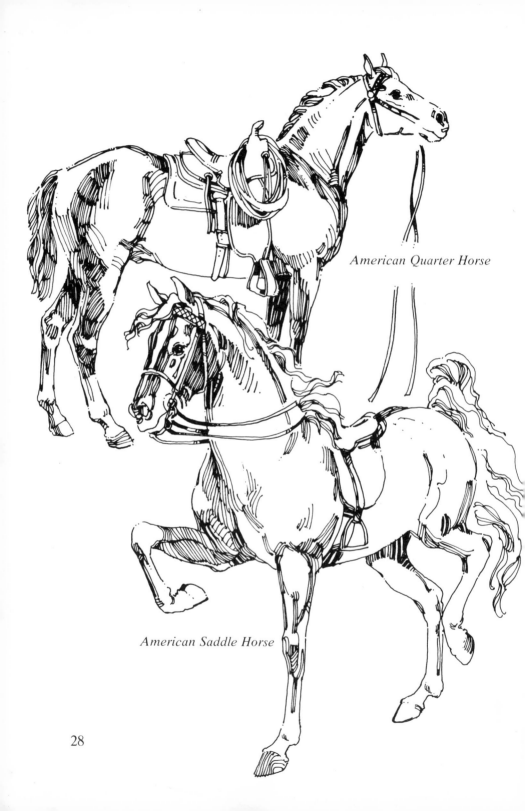

American Quarter Horse

American Saddle Horse

Shetland Pony

Hackney Pony

29

The Welsh pony averages about 50 inches (125 centimeters) in height and weighs about 500 pounds (225 kilograms). It is more spirited than the Shetland pony but does not have the Shetland's stubbornness. The Welsh pony makes a good jumper. Because it is strong and fast, it is an ideal pony for the advanced young rider.

With more young people becoming interested in riding, the pony has gained in popularity. Today there are more than a hundred pony clubs in the United States alone.

THE CHARACTERISTICS OF THE HORSE

How smart is a horse? To answer this question one must consider the instincts that the horse has inherited from its ancestors. The ancestors of the horse were not very well equipped to defend themselves. They did not have the long claws or the sharp teeth of a lion, nor did they have the deadly horns of a bull or the bite of a snake.

The horse's ancestors first hid from their enemies; later, as their legs grew longer, they outran them. Because of the horse's history of "fright and flight," some modern-day horses tend to be shy, nervous animals, quick to run at the first sign of danger. Some people think this is the action of a cowardly animal; actually the horse is responding to its natural instincts.

The horse's remarkable memory is, perhaps, the best sign of its intelligence. A horse forgets nothing. It remembers every path and road it has traveled. Give a horse its head and it somehow will find its way home even when the rider cannot. A horse seldom forgets the person who has beaten or mistreated it; it probably will dislike that person the rest of its life.

The horse is also a creature of habit. This trait, in addition to an exceptional memory, can add up to a few problems. Years ago, no one would buy a horse that once had pulled a fire engine. The buyer feared that this animal would take off at a gallop every time it heard a fire bell. Even today people find it almost impossible to change the habits of the Thoroughbred racehorse. This animal, because of its training, runs at top speed even when its racing days are over.

Even though horses are intelligent animals, the time required for training them is longer than that for other animals. The horse's timid nature and its great dignity will not allow it to give its trust and affection easily. Only after a long period will a horse overcome its instinctive fear of human beings. Only then will it be able to return affection and to learn.

Hackney ponies and Percherons are good examples of the degree to which horses can be trained. Both of these animals are excellent performers in the arena of a horse show or circus.

Horses, like people, are individuals. Some are very

bright, and some are less intelligent. Ponies are usually smarter than other horses; they are clever at getting their own way. To break this stubbornness, the trainer must show the pony that he or she is boss from the start. Once the pony realizes this, it can be trained to be a good mount and a close friend.

LEARNING TO RIDE

When you decide that horses are for you, you will probably want to take riding lessons. The bridle path or trail is not the best place to learn how to ride, however. Learning should take place in an enclosed area or paddock and under the supervision of an instructor or an experienced friend.

You should start your training with an English saddle. (Beginners are usually schooled in the English style of riding.) Later you can learn to ride western.

By no means should you learn on an animal that is skittish, bad-tempered, or partly broken. Beginners are not prepared to control such animals. You should, instead, learn on a well trained animal, which will help you be calm and relaxed. There is nothing to fear from a mount that has been ridden many times before and thus knows what to expect.

Mounting the pony or horse is quite simple. Stand on the animal's near side (the left side) with the reins gathered in your left hand. Keep the reins slack as long

Western Bridle

English Bridle

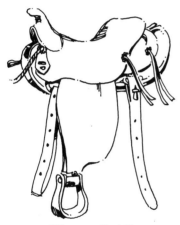

Western Saddle

English Saddle

as the pony or horse stands still. But if it moves while you are trying to mount, step down and pull the reins sharply as you say "whoa." When your mount is still, put your left foot in the stirrup. With your left hand, hold onto the front of the saddle and the reins as you hold onto the back of the saddle with your right hand. Pull yourself up and, while standing in the left stirrup, swing your right leg high over the animal's rump and gently settle into the saddle. Put your right foot in the right stirrup. To dismount do these steps in reverse.

Once in the saddle, sit up straight and take the reins in both hands. Your hands should be about six inches (15 centimeters) apart and close to the animal's withers. Your calves, knees, and thighs should be snug against the pony or horse and positioned under your body for good balance. The stirrup iron should be at the ball of your foot, not back against your heel. Bend your ankles in order to point the toes up and in.

To tell your mount what you want it to do, you must give it signals. Signals are given by pulling on the reins with your hands, applying pressure with your legs and heels, and giving voice commands. To get the animal to start slowly, apply pressure with your legs or gently tap its sides with your heels.

Turning a pony or horse is a little like steering a bicycle; with the reins, swing its head the direction you want it to turn. To go right, pull gently on the right rein. To go left, pull gently on the left rein. Use a firm, smooth pull. Jerking the reins only confuses the animal and hurts its mouth. To stop your mount, say "whoa" and gently pull back on the reins. Very little pressure is needed to let the animal know you want it to stop. Shifting your weight to the rear of the saddle also helps.

Practice starting, turning, and stopping in a ring until you are good at signaling your mount. When the horse is used to obeying your commands, you are ready to signal it to faster gaits.

The trot is a springy, bouncy gait. To sit a trot is very uncomfortable for a rider. Bumps and jolts can be avoided if the rider alternately stands up in the stirrups and then sits down in time with the horse's movements. This is called "posting."

The canter is a bit faster than the trot. It is a very comfortable, rolling gait that should give the rider a feeling of being in a rocking chair. Instead of posting, as with the trot, the rider leans forward slightly at the hips and stays seated in the saddle. The fastest gait is the gallop. Only experienced riders should gallop their horses.

Once you have learned to walk, trot, and canter your horse, you have acquired the basic skills of riding. You have learned to control your mount and to treat it with respect. You have learned to ride with head up, back straight, and arms tucked close to your body.

At this point in your development, you also should have learned that good manners are part of the responsibility of riding a horse. You should never gallop past other riders. Doing so may cause their mounts to shy or run away. Always go around other horses on the left side. Don't let your mount graze while you are riding, and don't ride across another person's land without permission. Rest your mount once in a while on a long ride. And always walk your mount the last 10 or 15 minutes of a ride; never bring it home in a sweat. Good riding manners make riding safer and more fun for you, your fellow riders, and your horse.

A HORSE OF YOUR OWN

Some boys and girls are fortunate enough to own a horse or pony. But most people ride horses rented from riding stables, which is the easiest and least expensive way for them to enjoy riding. This arrangement is good for those merely interested in weekend riding.

At the riding stables these people find their mounts all saddled and ready to go. Most of the time they ride in a line of nine or ten other riders. The horses are usually old and low in spirit, so the trail boss does not have to waste time in matching a horse to a rider's ability. After everyone is mounted, the trail boss starts off down the trail on a lead horse, followed by all the other horses. The trail winds through a farmer's pasture and somehow ends up back at the stable just as the allotted time runs out. The riders then jump down from their mounts, get into their cars, and drive home.

Of course, not all riding stables are quite like this. Some stable hands do try to match the rider's skill to the horse's temperament. But they are primarily interested in providing people with horses that will give them slow, safe rides for an hour or two.

Once you know how to ride, you probably will begin

thinking of a horse of your own. If you want to buy a horse, you should first ask yourself if you are genuinely interested in horses or if you enjoy riding only on the weekend. There is a difference. The expense and hard work of owning a horse can be justified only by a great love of horses. Horse owners spend more time grooming and saddling their horses than they do riding them. Owning a horse carries with it the important responsibility of seeing that the animal is properly cared for. Like any other domestic animal, a horse must be fed daily and trained.

Buying a horse is a serious and expensive undertaking. The initial price of a horse is only a small part of the total cost of owning the animal. The greatest expense will be keeping the horse at a boarding stable. This can cost from $75 to $150 a month, depending on the stable you choose. In addition to this expense, you will need a saddle and bridle. There will be veterinary fees and travel expenses. And you may wish to hire an instructor to teach you the correct way to train your horse and to ride.

If you are seriously interested in buying a pony or horse, you should make a point of meeting as many horsepeople as possible at riding stables and horse shows. These people usually know someone who has a horse for sale, or they can give you the name of a good breeder. And sooner or later young people out-grow their mounts and must sell them. If you buy someone else's horse, make sure it is in good health and not spoiled or bad-tempered.

Ponies and horses can also be obtained at auctions where they are sold to the highest bidders. These sales are too fast to allow you time enough to know what you are buying. Breeding farms have good selections of horses and ponies and are better places to buy. Most breeders are honest people with a real interest in horses. Reliable breeders will answer any questions you might have and will give you all the time you need to examine the pony or horse you are interested in. Good breeders will guarantee the health of the animal and will tell you which immunization shots it has had. But before making your purchase, you should have the pony or horse examined by a veterinarian.

Make sure that the horse you buy is well-broken. Stallions are usually too strong and high-strung for beginners. Mares tend to be more gentle, but some may be skittish. For those not interested in breeding horses, geldings make excellent mounts. Geldings are male horses that have had operations to prevent them from becoming fathers. Geldings usually are quiet, dependable animals. They do not have the hot temperament of stallions, nor do they have the nervousness of mares. In addition, geldings are quite easy to train.

Unless you are experienced in riding and training, you should buy a pony or horse that is at least three years old and fully trained. A trained animal will cost more than a young, untrained one, but the difference in price will be worth it to you.

The price of the pony or horse will depend not only upon its degree of training but also upon its breed and whether it is registered. A registered purebred pony or horse will cost more than an unregistered animal. If, however, you are not interested in showing your mount at horse shows, an animal bought for its merits will cost far less than a pedigreed animal. Such an animal will cost about $250. A new saddle and bridle will cost from $75 to $300, depending upon the quality. A used outfit can be had for as little as $35 and will do almost as well. More important than the cost of the saddle is its size.

If it doesn't fit the animal properly, it is of no value.

The size of your mount is another important factor to consider. Even though it has finished growing, you have not. If you buy a small pony that is the right size for you now, you probably will outgrow the animal within two years. You should, instead, buy a pony or small horse strong enough and big enough to carry a 15-year-old boy or girl. Unless you are very short, you should have little trouble handling an animal this size. It will carry you nicely until you are tall enough to ride a full-sized saddle horse.

Unless you live in the country, you will have to keep your mount at a boarding stable. Boarding stables are listed in the classified section of your phone book.

Visit several stables before you make a choice. The home for your pony or horse should be clean and roomy. Ideally it should have an arena for exercising horses indoors. The paddock should be free of weeds and trash. The surrounding countryside should offer interesting riding paths away from roads and traffic. Be sure the owner of the stable and the hired hands are friendly. As a rule, friendly people enjoy their work, which means they must like horses. They will treat your pony or horse with kindness and give it good care.

The stable hands will feed your mount and see that it gets fresh air and exercise. Unless other arrangements are made, your job will be to groom and saddle your pony or horse and to take care of its training.

HOUSING AND FEEDING

Boys and girls who keep their ponies or horses on their own property must know how to house and feed them. The stall does not have to be fancy or expensive. A corner of a barn 10 feet (three meters) square will do nicely. It should be clean, dry, and free of drafts. A dirt or clay floor is best. It should be covered with six inches (15 centimeters) of straw bedding, which will keep the horse or pony dry and warm when it feels like lying down. The bedding should be replaced twice a week, or whenever it becomes sticky or moist. But the stall should be cleaned out more often. You should use a shovel daily to take away the animal's waste.

A manger to hold hay should be provided at one end of the stall. A salt block should be available at all times —a pony or horse can lick as much as an ounce (28 grams) of salt a day. Water also must be available. An automatic water fountain will do away with the chore of carrying water to the stall. Otherwise, a water pail attached to the wall of the stall will do as long as it is kept filled.

All horses and ponies are likely to develop breathing problems if subjected to sudden changes of temperature. For a horse or pony to go out into the cold from a warm stall is not good for it. Neither would it be healthy for it to come into a warm stall from the cold outdoors. For your horse's or pony's health, it is best not to heat the stall during the winter months; ponies and horses grow heavy coats to protect them from the cold. As long as they are not in drafts, the cold will not affect them.

Your barn or stable should have a small room for storing feed and bedding. This room should have a concrete floor to protect the feed and bedding from moisture and mice and rats. Two or three cats will keep your stable free of rodents. If possible, have a small room for storing your saddles and bridles. This tack room should be closed off from the rest of the stable to keep your equipment free of dust.

Fenced-in pastures and paddocks intended for horses sometimes need altering when used for ponies. Usually the bottom strand of fence wire is too high. Ponies are clever at crawling under things and running off, but this can be prevented by stringing heavy wire halfway between the ground and the first strand of the fence. Do not use barbed wire; the pony could cut itself on the barbs.

The staple of any horse's or pony's diet is grass in the summer and hay in the winter. Timothy, alfalfa, and clover are the most common kinds of hay used for feed. Hay comes baled in two sizes. The large three-wire bale weighs more than a hundred pounds (about 45 kilograms) and is too heavy to lift. The two-wire bale weighs about 45 pounds (about 25 kilograms) and is easier to handle. The hay should be sweet-smelling, dry, and free of dust. Moldy hay can make a horse or pony very ill. It is just as poisonous as hay sprayed with insecticides.

Keep in mind that hay catches fire easily. Do not let anyone smoke or use matches in or around the stable or feed room. Also, do not combine a garage and a stable, which, in most states, is against the law. Not only can gasoline engines cause fires, but they can also poison animals with their exhaust fumes.

In the spring, ponies and horses should be fed a little hay each morning before they are turned out to pasture. This will prevent them from overeating the juicy

new pasture grass. While ponies and horses are grazing, they need water. A water pail should be attached to a strong post. A salt block should also be available. Get salt licks made especially for pastures. They have holes in them and can be placed over a post stuck in the ground.

Besides hay or grass, full-size horses should have grain in their daily diet. The standard grain used for feed is crushed or rolled oats. Corn is another grain sometimes fed in place of oats, but corn can be fattening.

Ponies usually do not have to eat any grain. They get along nicely on just hay or grass. If a pony is old or has been ridden hard, however, it needs a small amount of grain (about a handful twice a day). This will help keep the animal in good condition. Grain supplies a lot of extra energy, but too much grain can make your pony too frisky for you to handle. Do not feed grain unless it is recommended by your veterinarian or your trainer.

Ponies and horses love carrots, potatoes, and apples. Some people use these treats to get acquainted with the animals. Ponies and horses, however, are creatures of habit. If hand feeding is done too often, they come to expect choice tidbits every time they see humans coming. They may nip or kick if disappointed. It is best if this habit is never started.

GROOMING

Proper grooming is necessary in order to keep a horse or pony in good condition. It is also a good way to get to know your mount and to let it accustom itself to your touch. The animal should be groomed once a day if possible. After it has been ridden, it should be cooled off and groomed once more. Regular brushing and cleaning will keep a horse's or pony's oil and sweat glands open and working properly. This assures a healthy, glossy coat.

Grooming is made easier if the animal is kept in place by cross ties. These are straps or chains that go from each side of the halter to a wall or post.

In order to do a good job of grooming, you will need the following tools: hoof pick, currycomb, dandy brush, tail and mane comb, and body brush.

Begin the job of grooming by picking clean the pony's or horse's feet with a hoof pick. Getting a pony or horse used to having its feet lifted is a part of its

early training. Have your instructor or an experienced friend show you how to use the hoof pick. When working on your mount's feet, always face toward the rear of the animal. Never stand in back of it; if it is startled it may kick you. Always stand at the side of the animal where it can keep an eye on all your movements.

After the hooves are picked clean, remove the top dust from the coat by wiping it with a towel or cloth. Then go over the animal with a currycomb, starting at the front and working toward the rear. The currycomb loosens dirt from within the coat. Now use the dandy brush to remove this dirt. Next clean and brush the tail and mane with the tail and mane comb and the dandy brush.

Now go over the pony's or horse's entire body with the body brush. Brush in the direction the hair lies, not against it. Use the body brush in your right hand and keep the currycomb in your left hand. After four or five strokes of the brush, clean it with the currycomb. Finish the job by wiping down the animal with a towel or clean cloth. The pony's or horse's coat will look clean and shiny if you have done a thorough job. To complete grooming, wipe the pony's or horse's eyes and the area around its tail with a damp sponge.

Soap and water are seldom used on a horse or pony. Soap removes the natural oils from the animal's coat and leaves it dull and dry. But once in a while, during hot weather, a horse or pony will enjoy a shower bath from the garden hose. After showering your horse, dry it with a tool called a sweat scraper and towels.

Never groom a wet horse or pony. Animals damp from perspiration must be cooled off first, then dried and groomed. They should not be allowed to drink water until they have stopped breathing hard and have cooled completely. Always walk your pony or horse for the last 15 minutes of your ride; the animal then will return to the stable dry and cool instead of wet and hot. A sweaty horse is likely to catch cold if it isn't cooled properly.

During the winter your mount's coat will grow thick and heavy to protect it from the cold weather. This shaggy coat will be shed in the spring.

The outside of a pony's or horse's hoof is called the wall. The wall never stops growing. It, therefore, must be trimmed and filed every six weeks. This is done with a hoof nipper and a rasp, and is another job best done by an experienced person.

As a rule, ponies do not have to wear horseshoes. This is because ponies do not carry as much weight as horses and because their hooves are thicker and stronger than horses' hooves. The only time a pony must be shod is when it runs on hard surfaces such as paved highways. If your pony or horse wears shoes, they must be checked every five or six weeks to assure a good fit. The growing walls of the pony's or horse's hooves make frequent checking necessary.

THE BIRTH OF A FOAL

If you own a mare, you may decide to have her bred so that she can have a foal. The birth of a foal is an exciting experience. When your mare gives birth, you have the choice of keeping the foal or selling it. There are always buyers for a good pony or horse. You may wish to train the colt or filly for a year or two and then sell it; a trained animal brings an even better price. Besides, training a young animal is good experience for you.

When you have decided to have your mare bred, you must find a good stallion to be the father. For the use of the stallion, you must pay a stud fee. This fee can be very expensive, especially for an outstanding stallion. If your mare is unregistered, you may not want to spend a lot of money for stud fees, but you should use the best stallion you can afford. That way the foal will be at least as good as your mare and probably better. Because mares are easier to handle, it is customary to take the mare to the stallion to be bred.

Every 21 days a mare comes into heat. Only during these periods of heat will she mate with a stallion. The foal will be born 11 to 12 months after mating. Before the birth, your mare should have plenty of fresh air and exercise. She can be ridden until three months before foaling (giving birth).

Your mare probably will be able to foal without outside help. During birth, the foal should come out of the birth canal front feet first with the head tucked between its feet. If any other part of the foal appears before the front feet, the mare may have trouble giving birth. If the foal is in the wrong position, call your veterinarian. The doctor will turn the foal to make the birth safer and easier for the mare.

The foal arrives surrounded by a membrane sac and attached to its mother by an umbilical (uhm-BIL-uh-cul) cord. Through this cord the foal received nourishment while inside its mother. In its struggle to be born, the foal breaks the cord and tears the sac open. The foal is born with its eyes open and with a rough coat of

hair. It appears clumsy and misshapen as it struggles to stand on its long, wobbly legs. The cannon bones, or lower leg bones, are nearly the size they will be when the foal is grown.

Instinct tells the foal it must find its mother's milk bag, or udder, and start nursing. But sometimes the mare, especially one that has foaled for the first time, is so proud of her accomplishment that she insists upon nuzzling and smelling her new baby. All this attention prevents the foal from nursing, a predicament that calls for your help. Have someone steady the mare while you guide the foal to its mother's udder. Once the foal has nursed, it will not have trouble finding its next meal.

Make a point of touching the foal from the moment it is born. This will show it that it has nothing to fear from you or any other human. During the first few days, visit the foal often. Speak to it softly and gently stroke its body. Get it used to having its feet lifted. Within a week or two, you and the foal should be great friends. Later it will be ready to accept a halter and start its training.

TRAINING

Training a pony or horse is easier if you understand the animal's instincts. Wild ponies and horses once lived in herds on open plains. They were free to run and graze. They had little or no contact with human beings. In training a pony or horse, you are trying to get it to trust you enough to enable it to overcome its natural instincts. You are trying to accustom it to a world of narrow stalls, bits and bridles, saddles and riders—all things that are strange to it.

This means you must use patience and understanding instead of force and punishment. Using a whip or any other cruel device succeeds only in frightening the animal and making it bad-tempered. Horses and ponies are seldom born with mean dispositions; a bad-tempered animal is usually the result of poor training.

Many times a pony owner will say, "My pony is so stubborn, I can't train it." What this person really means is, "My pony is so smart that it wants to have its own way all the time." Once you understand that a pony's stubbornness (and laziness) is the result of its cleverness, you can go about controlling and correcting its behavior. Again, use patience, but let it know you are boss.

If you are training a horse or pony for the first time, ask the help of an experienced horseperson. Brushing off riders, kicking, biting, and rearing are faults that easily can be corrected by an experienced trainer. In order to train a pony or horse completely, you must get it used to people and to human touch, teach it to wear a halter, get it to lead, train it to longe, get it accustomed to a bit, break it to saddle, and get it used to carrying a rider.

Teaching a pony or horse to lead means teaching it to follow you as you lead it around by its reins or at the end of a short rope. It must not pull back or run ahead, and it must stop on command.

After the pony or horse has learned to lead, teach it to stand tied. Tie it to a ring attached to a wall. This sounds simple, but some horses and ponies do not like to be tied. Sometimes they even throw themselves on the ground to show their disapproval. Be sure the rope is long enough to allow your horse to reach the ground.

Do not do too much at one time. Use patience. Coax the animal; do not force it. A pony or horse enjoys praise and caresses. Talk to it softly. Tell it how proud

you are of its progress. Pat its neck and flanks to show affection. Once the pony or horse is accustomed to standing tied, it can be introduced to cross ties. Cross-tie it for a few minutes several times a day until it becomes comfortable with the process. Lift its feet often to get it used to having its hooves cleaned and shod.

In longeing, the pony or horse is taught to move in a circle at the end of a long rope. If done properly, longeing can be one of the most important steps in training. It gets the animal used to voice commands. It helps the pony or horse develop smooth, relaxed gaits. And it provides good exercise.

Longeing is a job for two people, one of whom should be very experienced. In longeing, one person holds the longe rope and a training whip while the other person leads the pony in circles.

For ponies, the longe line should be about 15 feet long; for horses, a little longer. The training whip should be the length of the longe line. The whip is used to accentuate commands and is *not* a tool for punishment. Touch the animal only occasionally with the whip.

Longeing can be fun for you and your pony or horse. As the animal trots or canters in response to your commands, you feel just like the animal trainer in a circus. Through proper longe training, your mount can be taught to respond to such voice commands as "walk," "trot," "canter," and "whoa." It is especially important that your pony or horse learn early in its education the meaning of "whoa;" it must stop immediately upon hearing this command. After months of longe training, you can teach your pony or horse to turn and move in the opposite direction simply by saying "change." Longeing is very helpful if done correctly.

Teaching a pony or horse to pull a cart is a good way to get it used to having a bit in its mouth and responding to pressure on the reins. Like longeing, this training can be done while the animal is still too young for riding.

The pony or horse can be broken to saddle when it is about two and a half years old. Because a pony or horse is afraid of new and strange objects, breaking it to saddle should be done gently and slowly. Let the pony or horse smell the saddle so that it knows it has nothing to fear. Put the saddle on the animal several times without cinching the girth. Next cinch the girth very loosely and let the pony or horse walk around a few minutes carrying the empty saddle. Do this several times. Soon the pony or horse will accept the strange thing strapped around its middle. Hold the reins in your right hand as you walk on the left side of the animal. This side, called the "near side," is the side from which all handling is done. After a few days of leading from the near side, the pony or horse will be accustomed to seeing you there.

The pony or horse is now ready to be ridden. Tighten the girth. Use a snaffle bridle. Have someone stand in front of the animal and hold its head by placing a hand on each side of the bit. Now, talking softly to your mount and patting its neck, climb into the saddle. Sit for a minute or two and dismount. Do this several times to show the pony or horse you have no intention of hurting it.

While sitting in the saddle, ask your assistant to lead the animal around the arena or paddock for a few minutes. Then ask him or her to let go and get out of the way slowly. Ride the pony or horse at a walk for a few minutes and then dismount. This is enough saddle-breaking the first day. Make each lesson as pleasant as possible by being gentle and patient with your mount.

Once in a while a pony or horse, especially a spirited stallion, will not let itself be broken easily. Such an animal should be broken by a strong, experienced rider who will stay in the saddle even when the horse rears. If the animal succeeds in throwing its rider once, it will rear and buck every time someone gets on its back. A spirited mount, especially, must learn that the rider is boss.

In disciplining your mount, you will be disciplining yourself as well. You and your horse, while partners in discipline, will also be partners in pleasure. The hard work of training your horse and caring for it will be paid back a thousand times as the two of you explore plains, woods, and valleys together. And the discipline and hard work of owning a horse probably will add up to a great love of horses on your part, a love that will further, by one step, the long partnership between horses and people.

HORSE TALK

Balk—to stop short; to refuse to obey

Bit—the part of the bridle that fits into the horse's mouth

Blaze—a large white streak down a horse's face

Bridle—the headgear by which a horse is controlled

Breaking—getting a horse used to a saddle and rider

Canter—a smooth gait a little slower than the gallop

Coat—the hairy skin of a horse

Colt—a young male horse

Crop—a small riding whip

Curry—to comb a horse's coat

Dam—a mother horse

Filly—a young female horse

Foal—a very young horse

Frog—the elastic, horny middle part of a horse's foot, shaped like a V

Gait—the forward movement of a horse, such as the walk, trot, canter, or gallop

Gallop—a gait in which the horse bounds forward in long strides; like a canter, only faster

Gelding—a neutered male horse

Halter—a set of straps placed around a horse's head and used for leading and tying up

Hand—a unit of measure used to describe a horse's height at the withers; one hand equals four inches (10 centimeters)

Longe line—a long rope used for training a horse

Mare—a grown-up female horse

Mount—to get on a horse (or a horse used for riding)

Paddock—a small fenced-in area for horses

Pony—any full-grown horse not more than 14.2 hands high

Rear—to rise up on the hind legs

Reins—lines attached to a horse's bit and held in the rider's hands

Shoes—metal plates fitted to the hooves to protect them from injury or wear

Shying—a sudden sideways movement of a horse due to fright

Socks—white leg markings on a horse

Sire—a father horse

Skittish—frightened easily, jittery

Stallion—a grown-up male horse able to be a father

Star—a small white patch on a horse's forehead

Tack—riding equipment, such as saddle and bridle

Trot—a gait slightly faster than a walk

THE PARTS OF A HORSE

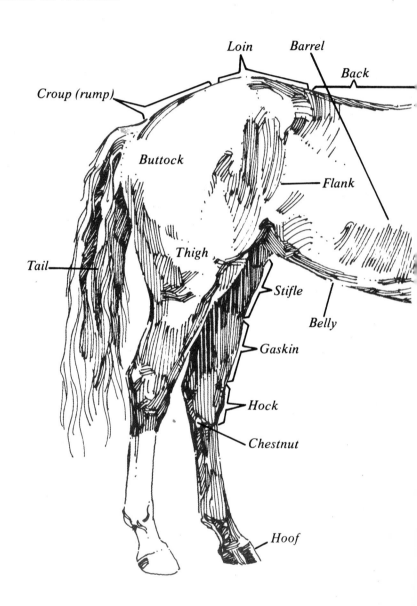

Loin

Barrel

Back

Croup (rump)

Buttock

Flank

Thigh

Tail

Stifle

Belly

Gaskin

Hock

Chestnut

Hoof

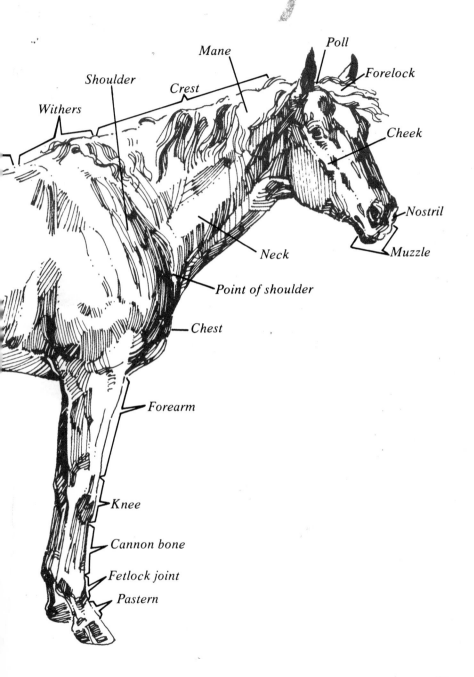

Withers

Shoulder

Mane

Crest

Poll

Forelock

Cheek

Nostril

Muzzle

Neck

Point of shoulder

Chest

Forearm

Knee

Cannon bone

Fetlock joint

Pastern

61

INDEX

You and Your Pet:

AQUARIUM PETS

BIRDS

CATS

DOGS

HORSES

RODENTS AND RABBITS

TERRARIUM PETS

We specialize in publishing quality books for young people. For a complete list please write

LERNER PUBLICATIONS COMPANY
241 First Avenue North, Minneapolis, Minnesota 55401